MW00437784

How to Become President without Really Lying

By G. Alan Penrod
Illustrated by Eric Boden

Dymon Publications
Printed in the U.S.A.

Author: G. Alan Penrod
Illustrations: Eric Boden
Editing: Linda Ferderer

Dymon Publications

ISBN 0-9637742-1-2

Printed in the U.S.A.

Disclaimer

There is no guarantee that by following these guidelines, you or your spouse will get a seat in the Oval Office. But hey, it's worked before, and you can't argue with success.

Intro

Seems like everyone wants to be President these days, and why not? The job requires that applicants meet only two qualifications* and brings all kinds of fringe benefits: free housing, world-class travel, paid vacation time, and a pretty decent salary to boot.

If you (or your spouse) have Presidential ambitions, this book is for you. It outlines the steps you need to take to get to the White House and is based on the success stories of people who have made it there recently.

*The age and native-born citizenship requirements are legally discriminatory, but who cares? Immigrants and people under 35 need not apply.

Getting there is only half the fun. If you can survive the election process and media scrutiny, then you're in for a real thrill as you maneuver your way through a gauntlet of public opinion polls, scandals, and their aftermath. But have no fear; current and previous Commanders-in-Chief have provided a blueprint for you to follow. This book reveals their hidden philosophies as well as techniques for dealing with personal indiscretions. You'll learn how to hedge, waffle, deny the truth, and ultimately stay in office, just like men of high and low caliber have done before you in their attempts to gain a place in America's history books.

Rewriting Your Past

Be born in a small town with a patriotic-sounding name like "Hope," "Liberty," or "Justice." Then, move out before you know what the word means. Make a big deal out of your birthplace, as if your being born there was more than mere coincidence.

Promise the hometown folks that if they put you in office, you will put them on the map. Some day you will use tax dollars to build a presidential library, and people will come from miles around to pretend they're interested.

Make everyone think your childhood was rough even if it wasn't. You can't afford to lose the sympathy vote.

Learn to pull the wool over people's eyes when you are young. Some of your best supporters will be those who say, "But he's such a *nice* boy. He would never do a thing like *that*."

If you get caught with your hand in the cookie jar, learn to say, "But I wasn't going to *eat* the cookie; I was just fondling it."

Find a way to believe your own lies so that you can convincingly tell them to others. Keep a sweet, innocent expression on your face and no one will suspect anything.

Learn to cover your tracks at a young age.

Become an actor.

When confronted with a moral dilemma, think, "How will this affect me if I run for President some day?" Then go ahead and do it anyway. You'll have plenty of time to fabricate excuses later on.

Keep your presidential ambitions in mind as you are growing up, so you can refine techniques for hiding youthful indiscretions.

Find a way to avoid the draft. You need to survive so you can send other people's kids to war.

Become a lawyer. Then you can weasel your way out of anything.

Learn to speak lawyer-ese. Then everybody will believe you're not deceiving anybody.

Make friends with lots of lawyers. They will make good advisors for you later on and will stand by you until they have to face up to scandals of their own.

Eliminate those distinguishing marks or they may some day eliminate you.

Learn how to promise all things to all people.

Learn how to spell "potato" without the "e".

Learn how to get teary-eyed on cue.

Learn how to swear like an (expletive deleted).

Learn to salute like a real veteran.

HOW DO WE GET TO WASHINGTON?

The Democratic Way
How to Get Elected, Then Lie about It

Try to campaign on a shoestring. You'll need the extra money for legal defense funds later.

Never say anything that can't be twisted to your advantage by spin doctors.

Appearances aren't everything. They're the only things that matter.

A cute smile for the cameras can hide a multitude of sins.

Take your show on the road.

Spy on the competition.

The best flood insurance is to avoid things with water in them:
Hot water, deep water, Whitewater, Watergate, Waterloo . . .

Never get on a boat called "Monkey Business."

Never be caught with your pants down. Have a plausible answer to "Boxers
or briefs?"

Make sure you cover-up your cover-ups.

Put a good whitewash in the spin cycle.

CAMPAIGN RALLY OF THE FAITHFUL

The media are more important than the message. Let them use you to your own advantage.

Pander like there's no tomorrow.

The best people to plant in the audience are insomniacs who will applaud in the right places.

Encourage third party candidates who can siphon off votes from your main opponent.

If you can't come up with a flat answer, waffle.

Promise change. Then change your promises.

Never champion a cause or group that you can't betray later.

Hire speech writers to come up with catchy campaign slogans that you don't intend to abide by. Some that probably won't work:

> Read my lips: No new faxes.
> It's the economy, Cupid. Keep your mind on the economy!
> Pot for every chicken.
> Ask not what you can do for your President. Ask how to keep it from the grand jury.
> Two liberals for the price of one, and at double the cost!
> Don't! Stop! Think about tomorrow!

MY OPPONENT'S UNSCRUPULOUS CHARACTER IS NOT AT ISSUE HERE.

In the Debates

Be liberal with underhanded jabs masquerading as compliments.

Try to throw a preachy one-liner into every statement you make.

Pretend to be pretending not to laugh at your opponent's answers.

Think of a good answer to questions like, "If the U.S. were at war, would you support equality in the draft, and if so, would you allow your daughter to be drafted?" Then pray that no one asks.

Come up with newfangled definitions, like "A family consists of one (or more) parents and one (or more) children." Disregard traditional values and married couples who happen to be childless.

Did I say that?   What I meant was . . .

Before the election: "No more taxes!"
After the election: "No! More taxes!"

Before the election: "Tax cut promised."
After the election: "Tax. Cut promise."

Before the election: "Taxes pending."
After the election: "Tax and spending."

Before the election: "I'll never raise taxes!"
After the election: "I need a raise. Taxes!"

MUCHAS ARIGATO

It's the Money, Honey

Before the election, raise money. After the election, raise taxes.

Get money from anyone willing to donate. Then make *contributors* take the fall if it turns out to be illegal. (You wouldn't have accepted if you had known. Yeah, right.)

If they don't offer, solicit.

Some folks won't contribute unless you ask in a foreign language.

The world makes money go round.

Bribery without money. Money without bribery:

      Auction off handshakes, photo-ops, and Presidential suites.

      Beds go to the highest bidders.

Never bite the hand that pays your way into office.

Give high profile government jobs to friends and relatives. Then they will do anything to keep you in power.

Always keep your cronies happy. They may have to defend you before a grand jury some day.

NOT EXACTLY TAKING THE OATH OF OFFICE.

Maxims to Live By

It's easier to give your word than to keep it.

Hide the truth today, and you'll be hiding from it tomorrow.

Ambiguity is the best way to keep people wondering.

Draw a fine line, but only after you've crossed it.

An excuse is never having to say you're sorry.

Always take credit when credit is due (to someone else).

It's more blessed to fib than to deceive.

Take responsibility for everything except your own actions.

"It's not my fault" should be implied if not said.

He who makes the rules, breaks the rules.

Never break a law that you can't deny later.

Never record (or videotape) what you can't erase.

Any fire that you put out today could reignite tomorrow.

Never admit your mistakes when you can blame them on someone else.

SIGNING THE TOBACCO BILL

If you sit higher on the totem pole, more people will look up to your butt.

Laws are made for the powerless.

Lofty ideals are like balloons; they can carry you above the law and above the fray.

Morals are for everybody else.

There's no limit to the good you can do, or the bad that can undo you.

No matter what you use as a cover-up, holes will eventually burn through.

A good way to bring down the cigarette industry is to smoke cigars or marijuana.

It takes guts to bask in others' glory.

Retaliation is the best way to get back at people.

If you can't baffle them with baloney, overwhelm them with insignificance.

No system is so well organized that a little government intervention can't foul it up.

The role of bureaucracy is to make it impossible for people to accomplish what they can easily do on their own.

Mindless paperwork and meaningless procedures should never get in the way of bureaucracy.

By Definition . . .

Character is a fictitious person.

Indecent exposure is what the media do when they catch you in one of your lies.

It's not adultery if you leave your shirt on.

It's not perjury if you say it with a sincere expression on your face.

It's not smoking if you use a joint or cigar.

It's not raising taxes, if you call it "contributions."

A little of this; a lot of that:

It wasn't indecent exposure, it was just a little show and tell.
It wasn't sex, it was just a little indecent exposure.
It wasn't adultery, it was just a little sex.
It wasn't an affair, it was just a little adultery.

You're not fooling anybody:

"I deny that it is true," really means "It is true that I am denying it."

"I didn't inhale," really means "I hope you're swallowing my story."

"I never had an affair with that woman," really means "We only had time for a few quickies. My wife was always nearby."

What's that you say?

Character? I saw it in a movie once.
Dignity? It died with chivalry.
Responsibility? My subordinates will take care of that.
Hypocrisy? I would never do a thing like that.
Backbone? My wife has one, I believe.
Trust? Isn't that something you put your money in?
Credibility? People don't believe in that anymore, do they?
Misconduct? Is there something wrong with that?
Competence? That's not my forte.
Integrity? Well, it all depends . . .

Backpedaling: The illegitimate child of back slapping and influence peddling.
Presidential privilege: 10% presidential and 90% privilege.

Don't Mess with the Economy, Stupid

Leave the economy alone. Then you can claim credit for doing absolutely nothing.

Make sure your predecessor has appointed the right person to the Federal Reserve Board. Then let him do his job. Try to make the media believe it was all your doing.

The best way to get the other party elected to Congress is to try and push your economic agenda.   Give the people a taste of the horrors they would experience with one-party rule.

Don't try to fix anything. Your solutions are worse than the original problem.

Become a centrist, but only after you've demonstrated what everyone knew all along: Your extremist policies would bring disaster if left unchecked.

Attack the wealthy, but only after you've soaked them for everything you can get.

Renege on tax promises early on, so people won't remember them when the next election rolls around.

Steal economic issues from the other party, but only after you've proven that your hair-brained ideas won't work.

Make the public think everything good was your doing and everything bad is Congress's. You're popularity depends on it.

THIS IS WHAT I CALL "SECRET SERVICE"

What to Do If You Get There
How to be a Square Peg in the Oval Office

Fulfill promises to special interest groups early in your presidency, so everyone will know how much you care about the majority.

Continue to campaign after you have won. It shows how much confidence you have in your mandate from the people.

Kowtow to extremists in your party. Weren't they the ones who got you elected?

To demonstrate your faith in public education, enroll your child in a private school.

Let someone else make the agenda. You have nothing important to say or do anyway.

Appoint cabinet members who are prone to corruption, so you will look good by comparison.

Get your picture taken next to historic figures and on historic occasions. Some day people will think you invented the photo-op.

Set an example for the children of America. Then they will grow up to be good adulterers.

Put your best face forward. Allow others to answer questions you should be answering yourself.

Be in the "right" place when you really should be somewhere else.

Improve your golf game. You should have something to show for all that time in (the) office.

Appoint ultra-liberals to government posts to fulfill your obligations to the vast minority.

Jog. Then everyone will see what type of jelly you're really made of.

Let it all hang out.

Fumble with the English language. Hammer the grammar until nobody, including yourself, really knows what you mean.

Prove to the public that when it comes to philandering, you're no JFK. Kennedy had class.

Make calls from the White House to "thank" potential donors in advance for their generous contributions.

Use the bureaucracy to your best advantage.

Secret Service: 2 bodyguards and 1,000 character guards

Give interns private tours in the Oval Office.

Use the presidential plane as a barber shop. Then the American people can see their tax dollars squandered in high places.

Surround yourself with high-priced lawyers, so your backers will see that they're getting their money's worth.

Withhold crucial information, so your press secretary will have something to hedge about.

Attack those who seek to destroy you. That's the best way to insure that they will.

Sic the IRS on anyone who opposes or exposes you.

Let he who is without stones, cast false allegations.

Go on the offensive whenever you see you are losing ground.

Dish out the truth in small increments, and only after you can't deny it anymore.

Let others pay the price, so you won't have to.

Learn to play the blame game.

Find out what the public thinks before taking a risky stance. Forget about personal convictions, as if you had any to begin with.

Bestow insignificant favors, so people will know how much you really care.

Save energy by napping in important meetings.

If you have bad news for one state, make the announcement well within the boundaries of its neighbor.

Always be seen espousing charitable causes, whether you support them in policy or not.

Puncture your own tires; then blame the leak on someone else.

When the going gets tough, bring out those emotions.

Comb through the FBI files for dirt on potential political opponents.

Use those White House coffees to get the campaign juices flowing.

Try to charm potential contributors and whistle-blowers.

Hiding the truth always pays
     hush money
     lawyers
     independent counsels
     talk shows
     book publishers.

Always give the media the impression that you are hiding something. Then they will hound you until they find out what it is. This will generate a lot of free publicity for your policies, which people have very little interest in.

Play hide-and-seek with incriminating memos, billing records, and money made from too-good-to-be-true investments.

Spouse-in-Chief

Choose your spouse well: a man whom you can manipulate, or a woman who will manipulate you.

Marry someone who wants to be President more than you do.

Behind every public man, there is a woman trying to push her own agenda.

Your wife can be your strongest supporter. Support her. She can turn the masses against you.

Fire anyone your wife doesn't like.

The best way to keep your wife from meddling in foreign policy is to have her speak out about topics she has no business getting into.

Transfer all questionable income into your spouse's name.

Let your wife experience the thrill of finding long lost documents at just the right time.

Before you move into the White House, make sure your wife has redecorated. Give her free reign in choosing Cabinets and allocating office space.

Assign your spouse an "unpaid" job that could end up costing the country billions of dollars.

Never get in your wife's way when she tries to run the country.

Relinquish power to your spouse. You are her co-President after all.

When the President hungers for glory and the First Lady hungers for power, the country hungers for real leadership.

All the political power in the world is a poor substitute for a faithful husband.

Keep your wife in the background where she can watch you like a hawk.

Fidelity is an old wives' tale.

Consult astrologers who can predict things that have already happened.

ROUGHING IT.

How Not to Be a Leader

Focus on yourself and your popularity. Make those polls count, even if you are irrelevant.

Be there when something important happens. That way, people will think you had a hand in it.

Invite real leaders from other countries to the White House. Crowds will gather to see them, and you can share their spotlight.

Let your wife handle everything. At least she knows what she wants.

Try to push policies which few people feel strongly about.

Just stay out of the way, and let the economy take care of itself.

Try to look and act Presidential, even if you are not.

Make sure you get invited to historical events.

Pray that there are no serious crises during your presidency which require true leadership. Then, the country will never have to find out what you're really made of.

People of strength, competence and conviction inspire others to emulate them. Good thing you aren't trying to lead us anywhere.

Are we following you, or are you following us?

Digging up dirt, or
digging a hole for yourself?

Keys to Staying in Office

Choose a vice-president who is more extremist than you are. Then no one will dare assassinate or impeach you.

When you've really blown it, put your wife on the front lines to defend you.

Have damage control teams that can clean up after each other.

Travel to foreign countries when the domestic fire gets hot.

Time your "no confidence" votes to occur during non-presidential election years.

How to divert attention from your follies:

Get a puppy.

Place undue attention on the economy.

Go abroad. People are kinder to you there.

Blame it all on conspiracy.

Let the media focus on your spouse's attire or hairstyle.

Pretend to be happily married.

Rather than honestly admitting your mistakes, lash out at critics and witnesses.

Try to get off on technicalities.

When the going gets tough, resort to

> Name calling: "I'm being hunted by a witch."
> Bribery: "Remember that job you wanted. . ."
> Fabrication: "Here's the story as you remember it."
> Threats: "If you tell the truth, you'll be sorry."
> Espionage: "Our private detectives are watching you."
> Blackmail: "If you expose me, I'll expose you."
> Extortion: "We know who your children are."

Excuses, excuses

"Presidents in the past have done the same thing."
>The great ones stood for the right rather than hiding from the wrong.

"I wanted to protect my family."
>If that were true, you would never have broken your vows in the first place.

"The American people hired me to do a job."
>Did the job description include shenanigans in the Oval Office?

"Everyone is out to get me."
>Of course they are. Catching eels is a challenging sport.

"There is no evidence to prove any wrongdoing."
>The evidence is within you. And you can never escape that.

Your Legacy

Be sure to make the news every day, for good or for evil. Then people will have something to remember you by.

You have accomplished more than your surgeon general ever could; you've prompted open discussions of sex in the public schools.

The children of America are getting quite an education in their current events classes, and it has little to do with the economy or good citizenship.

What you are, not what you profess to be, will determine how history treats you.

In the end, you will be remembered most by what you want to be least remembered by.

Your popularity is determined by what you do when the cameras are rolling Your legacy will be determined by what you do when they are not.

Some characters put on a good stage performance. Those *with* character don't need an audience in order to perform.

The country follows its leader. Be careful where you lead her.

A Final Word:

I Didn't Do It

I didn't do it. No Siree

I didn't chop the cherry tree

It wasn't I. It wasn't me.

I didn't smoke that tiny joint

A puff or two--that's not the point

I didn't inhale. Don't you see?

A war was on, and I was free!

That little room in Little Rock

A little show, a little talk

A little gal who didn't knock

And now the people, how they mock

I didn't do it. Yes, I swear it

All I did was grin and bear it.

I didn't kiss her on the lips

Or squeeze her tight or touch her hips

I didn't send her on those trips

Or get her jobs or give her scripts

I didn't tell her how to lie

And if you ask me, I'll deny

I'm not a crook

I'm not a wimp

I'm not a playboy

Not a pimp

No FDR, no Thomas J.

No Honest Abe, no JFK

Who were those people anyway?

I didn't take that foreign money

My hands were tied. Believe me, Honey

I didn't sell the Lincoln bed

I gave out jobs and perks instead

And in the morning when they woke

They came for coffee and we spoke

A photo-shoot for every caller

Another day, another dollar

I didn't say I'd cut your taxes

Read my lips now: No more axes

The budget's here; it's time to spend

Promises were made to bend

Just like the truth--if they can't prove it

You'll have some time to hide and move it

The lay. The lie

Delay. Deny

Deny the lay. Delay the lie

I didn't do it. No Siree

It wasn't I. It wasn't me.